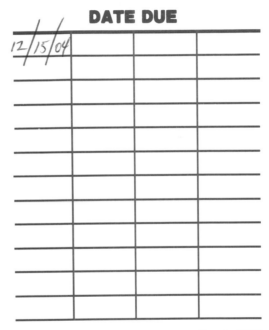

DATE DUE

12/15/04			

Demco No. 62-0549

Contemporary Hispanic Americans
DOLORES HUERTA

BY
FRANK PÉREZ

RSVP
**RAINTREE
STECK-VAUGHN**
P U B L I S H E R S
The Steck-Vaughn Company

Austin, Texas

Published by Raintree Steck-Vaughn, an imprint of Steck-Vaughn Company.
Produced by Mega-Books, Inc.
Design and Art Direction by Michaelis/Carpelis Design Associates.
Cover photo: Beth Corbin Photographer/Reprinted by permission of the National Organization for Women

Library of Congress Cataloging-in-Publication Data
Pérez, Frank, 1956–
    Dolores Huerta/by Frank Pérez.
        p.   cm.—(Contemporary Hispanic Americans)
    Includes index.
    Summary: Describes the efforts in the 1960s of Dolores Huerta to organize migrant workers in California into a union which became the United Farm Workers.
    ISBN 0-8172-3981-2 (Hardcover)
    ISBN 0-8114-9789-5 (Softcover)
    1. Huerta, Dolores, 1930-   —Juvenile literature. 2. Women labor leaders—United States—Biography—Juvenile literature. 3. Mexican Americans—Biography—Juvenile literature. 4. Trade-unions—Migrant agricultural laborers—United States—History—Juvenile literature. 5. United Farm Workers—History—Juvenile literature. [1. Huerta, Dolores, 1930-   . 2. Labor leaders. 3. Mexican Americans—Biography. 4. Women—Biography. 5. Migrant labor.] I. Huerta, Dolores, 1930-   . II. Title. III. Series.
HD6509.H84P47 1996
331.88'13'092—dc20
[B]   95-18207
                                                              CIP
                                                              AC
Printed and bound in the United States.

1 2 3 4 5 6 7 8 9 LB 99 98 97 96 95

Photo credits: A. Schatz: pp. 4, 25; Archives of Labor and Urban Affairs, Wayne State University: pp. 7, 8, 22, 31, 38; Courtesy Dolores Huerta: pp. 11, 12, 15, 16; UPI/Bettmann: p. 19; AP/Wide World Photos: pp. 21, 26, 33, 35, 37, 41, 42; Paul Fusco/Magnum: p. 29; Beth Corbin Photographer/Reprinted by permission of the National Organization for Women: p. 44.

Contents

Chapter *One*

A LIFE IN LABOR

My father was a labor union organizer. A labor union is an organization, or group, that works for and protects the needs of its working members. A union organizer is a person who starts and keeps a union together. My father's job was to help people get better pay and a safer workplace. In 1968, I took a trip with my father to Washington, D.C. We were not there to see the sights. My father had brought me with him to attend a rally of poor and working people from all over the country. I had been to other meetings and marches with him. But that day in Washington, D.C., was different—I had never seen 100,000 people in one place before!

At the rally, I heard some people in front of us shouting. "Give them room!" they yelled. Who were

Dolores Huerta has spent her life fighting for the rights of poor and working people. Here, she organizes farm workers in Delano, California, in the 1960s.

they talking about? Suddenly, the crowd parted and I saw a man and a woman. I asked my father who they were. He told me they were two very famous union organizers, Cesar Chavez and Dolores Huerta.

Later, I got to meet them. They did not act like they were famous. Actually, they seemed like most other people I knew. That was when I began to realize what sort of people farm workers and their leaders are. They are simple people. They are also strong survivors who believe very firmly in fair pay for hard work.

Dolores Huerta was one of the strongest leaders of the farm workers during the 1960s and 1970s. She dedicated her life to making the world a better place for people who had been left out of the American Dream. For these people, hard work had not added up to success. Farm workers were surrounded by food crops in the fields, yet their own families often went hungry. Dolores Huerta worked very hard for much of her life to change that.

With her friend Cesar Chavez, Dolores began a union for farm workers. This union is called United Farm Workers, or UFW. It has improved the lives of thousands of farm workers and their families.

Starting a union is very difficult. It was even more difficult for Dolores because she was a woman and a Mexican American. Women and minorities often have a hard time getting their demands met in American society. Dolores was also the mother of 11 children. She was often pregnant when she was working. At times,

Dolores Huerta was one of the few women leaders in the labor movement. At the first meeting of the farm workers' union in 1962, Dolores was elected vice president.

she was also a single parent. In the 1960s, most people believed a woman's place was at home, cooking and taking care of the children. This was especially true in the Mexican-American community. Yet Dolores did not allow such attitudes to slow her down.

Today, Dolores Huerta remains a strong role model for Hispanic-American women, who are often treated poorly because of their race and sex. Dolores's courage and leadership inspired many people. Lupe Ortiz, another union organizer, explained how important it was to see a woman in a leadership role: "We could see she was always out in front, and she would talk back. She wasn't scared of anything."

Dolores was arrested more than twenty times because of her political activities. Yet even going to jail did not compare to the life-threatening injury she suffered at a 1988 demonstration in San Francisco.

Because Dolores was "always out in front" in the struggle for justice, she became a role model for women.

Dolores was in a peaceful protest against the policies of George Bush. He was running for President at the time. During the protest, she was clubbed by police officers and rushed to the hospital. During emergency surgery, her spleen was removed. She also suffered six broken ribs. Even from her hospital bed, however, Dolores helped change the laws. The police had to change the way they controlled crowds so that what had happened to Dolores would never happen again.

Today, Dolores is one of the highest-ranking women in the U.S. **labor movement**. Some people might think that an important and powerful woman like Dolores would be rich as well as famous. Nothing could be further from the truth. Everyone at the UFW works as a volunteer, which means that no one is paid a salary. The union just pays for its staff's rent, food, and medical expenses. "It has always been our philosophy that you cannot help farm workers if you are so much richer than they are," Dolores once wrote. Her work with the union may not have made Dolores money, but it did win many gains for the farm workers for whom she fought.

Dolores's climb to the top was not an easy one. But it was always fueled by a sense of commitment that began when Dolores was still a young girl.

Two

GROWING UP

Dolores Fernandez was born in the mining town of Dawson, New Mexico, on April 10, 1930. It was a very hard time for Dolores's family and for most Americans. About six months before Dolores's birth, the U.S. economy fell apart. During the 1930s, millions of Americans were out of work. This period in American history is called the Great Depression. Many families were homeless and forced to live on the streets.

Dolores's father, Juan Fernandez, was a miner. He worked deep inside mountains, digging out minerals. When he was not working in the mines, he worked in the fields. Like other farm workers, he often spent 12 to 16 hours a day in the hot sun picking fruits and vegetables. The workers were paid very little for this backbreaking work. Many farm workers were Mexican Americans. Most of them had little or no schooling, and some did not speak English. They also had to face prejudice.

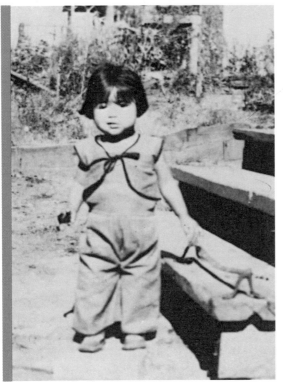

Dolores Fernandez in
New Mexico in 1931.

There was no security in farm work. When farm
workers were finished harvesting a crop, their job was
done. Then they had to move to another farm, where
there was work, and start all over again. This is why
farm workers were also called **migrant workers**.
Because they moved so often, it was hard for them to
feel that they belonged to a community.

Mr. Fernandez traveled to Colorado, Nebraska, and
Wyoming for the beet harvests. The bad **working
conditions** angered him. He wanted to help improve
things for people like himself. Little did he know that

Dolores poses with her mother, Alicia; stepfather, James Richards; and brothers, Marshall and John. Alicia Fernandez Richards taught young Dolores to treat all people with respect.

his own daughter would one day lead the fight to end these terrible working conditions.

In 1936, Dolores's parents divorced. Her father stayed in New Mexico to work. Dolores and her two brothers, John and Marshall, went with their mother, Alicia, to Stockton, California. There they lived in a poor, ethnically and racially mixed neighborhood, with Hispanic, Japanese, Italian, Jewish, and African Americans. All these different people made Dolores's neighborhood a very interesting place to live. Alicia Fernandez raised her daughter to respect everyone, no matter where they came from or what religion they practiced. In Stockton, Dolores's mother worked in a canning factory and also as a waitress. Dolores was often cared for by her grandfather.

Dolores was a pretty girl with dark eyes and long black hair. Her dark skin showed her father's Mexican-Indian heritage more than her mother's Spanish blood. Dolores was very playful, despite her family's hardships during the Depression. And she loved to talk! "My grandfather used to call me 'seven tongues'," Dolores recalls, "because I always talked so much." Later, Dolores took music and dancing lessons, sang in her church choir, and began to write poems and stories. She was also a girl scout for many years.

Alicia Fernandez saved all her money and started her own restaurant. Later, she bought a hotel with her second husband, James Richards. The hotel guests were mostly farm workers and other hardworking people. Dolores saw that her mother's business was making good money. This way she learned that women could be as successful as men.

As a child, Dolores did not see much prejudice, since there were so many different kinds of people in her community. Also, her mother's own beliefs helped Dolores see everyone as an equal. It was not until

Dolores was in high school that she experienced racism firsthand.

At that time, during World War II, there were many violent fights in Los Angeles between groups of soldiers and groups of young Hispanic-American men. These events fueled prejudice against all Hispanic Americans. Dolores felt the tension at her high school in Stockton. People began to treat her differently. "I started noticing racism as a teenager and it took a long time to get over the feelings," Dolores recalls. It was a painful experience for her.

In school Dolores was a good student. But her good work there was not always trusted. She recalls that in one of her classes she got all A's on her papers and tests, but she got a C for the class. She asked the teacher why she received such a low grade. The teacher said that her work was too good, and that someone else must have written her papers for her! Dolores was very hurt. Her teacher believed that just because Dolores was Mexican-American she could not be smart.

Another time, there was a contest to see which student could sell the most war bonds. Whoever sold the most bonds would receive a special trophy. Dolores sold the most bonds, but she never got the prize. "They could not face the fact that a Mexican-American girl had sold the most," she later said.

At the same time that Dolores was coping with prejudice at school, her mother was helping people

As a Mexican American, Dolores faced racism during her school years. She learned to hate prejudice and injustice.

who were having a tough time. Alicia often let the poor farm-worker families stay at her hotel for free. Like Dolores's own father, these men and women worked hard in the fields for very little money. Still, they could not afford shelter. It was not fair. Dolores wanted to help them.

Her chance to fight prejudice came soon enough. Dolores was in a club at school that was planning a school dance. Some of the club members wanted to charge each student three dollars to get in. Dolores knew that many students could not afford a three-dollar admission charge. She suggested that the club

charge less money. But other club members did not care if poorer students could not afford to go. Dolores was so mad about this that she quit the club.

Dolores did not let these setbacks stop her from finishing high school. In fact, Dolores went on to study at Stockton College. This was an unusual step for women of her time and background.

Dolores took a break from her college studies to marry her high school sweetheart, Ralph Head. They had two daughters, Celeste and Lori. The marriage did not work out, and Dolores and Ralph were divorced. Dolores returned to school and earned an associate's degree. Her mother helped her out by baby-sitting and paying some of the bills.

At that time, Dolores had many different jobs. First, she managed a grocery store. Then, she worked as a secretary at a naval supply base. She also worked in the sheriff's office. None of these jobs made her happy, so she went back to school to study teaching. She felt that through teaching, she could help improve people's lives.

Dolores soon became a teacher. Many of her young students came from poor, farm-working families. Dolores found that these children needed more than an education. They and their families needed food and clothes as well. Dolores became frustrated. Dolores realized that even as a teacher she "couldn't do anything for the kids who came to school barefoot and hungry," she explained later.

As a teen, Dolores had not been able to just stand by and watch injustice. Now, as an adult, she knew she had to take serious action. She wanted a chance to help the farm workers and their families. With the help of an organization called the CSO, Dolores got her chance.

Chapter

DISCOVERING HER LIFE'S WORK

In 1955, Dolores met a man named Fred Ross. Fred worked for a group called the Community Service Organization (CSO), which was created to help Mexican Americans build better lives for themselves.

Fred Ross traveled from town to town to set up new chapters, or local groups, of the CSO. At first, Dolores could not believe that a non-Hispanic was really interested in helping farm workers. She looked into his background and discovered that he was sincere. Dolores began listening to what he had to say.

The lives of the workers in Stockton were difficult. Many lived in tents or shacks with dirt floors. There was no running water or indoor toilets. Children had to work to help support their families, so they often could not go to school. And when they were not working, the children had no safe places to play.

The CSO believed it could help the Mexican-American farm workers through voter registration and

Farm workers received very little pay for their long hours of backbreaking work. Here, strawberries are picked by farm workers in Salinas, California, in 1963.

citizenship classes. Many Mexican Americans did not vote in elections. Yet there were huge numbers of Mexican-American farm workers in California alone. If they all voted together, they could elect politicians who would fight for their rights.

The first step for the CSO was to register, or sign up, farm workers to vote. This was not so easy. Many workers moved too often to be able to vote in one place. Many of them did not read or write English well, so they could not pass the tests they had to take before they could vote. Others could not prove they were United States citizens.

To help, the CSO taught the workers to read and write English and get citizenship papers so they could vote. But many of the farm workers were afraid to register. They thought they might lose their jobs if their bosses found out they could vote. The growers who owned the farms did not want their workers to have voting power. They did not want to pay workers more money or build better housing for them, either. In fact, sometimes the growers would hire people to beat up the farm workers and their organizers.

So it was not surprising that the farm workers did not trust outsiders like Fred Ross. The first thing Fred had to do when he came into a new town was to win the workers' trust. First, he set up a "house meeting" at the home of one of the workers. This way people would feel comfortable and not be afraid to talk. The idea of having house meetings came from the farm workers themselves. Fred was talking to a group of workers. Dolores recalled someone saying, "Look, let's go over to my friend's house and we'll meet there with some of the other workers."

Dolores first met Fred Ross at a meeting where he talked about what people could do if they worked together for their rights. Fred wanted to set up a chapter of the CSO, and he needed volunteers to help him. This was exactly the kind of work Dolores had been hoping to do.

When she told her fellow teachers what she was going to do, their reaction was not surprising. After all, here was a single mother with children to support, giving up a good job with benefits. At first, Dolores said, "The other teachers that I worked with thought I was crazy. Later on, though, they thought it was wonderful."

Dolores joined the CSO. She began as a volunteer going door-to-door to help register people to vote. She also met another man who would help to change her life. His name was Cesar Chavez. Chavez was a Mexican American and a farm worker. He had started working for the CSO as a volunteer, just like Dolores. The two shared a common goal: to get justice for the farm workers. From the beginning, they were dedicated, hard workers, but they had a lot to learn. Fortunately,

Cesar Chavez became a hero to workers everywhere and a lifelong friend and colleague to Dolores Huerta.

As a lobbyist, Dolores Huerta pushed for new laws to help the farm workers. Here, she meets with Assemblyman John Moreno at the California State Capitol in Sacramento.

Fred Ross was a good teacher. Fred taught the pair how to speak to large gatherings of people and, most important, how to win people's trust.

Dolores and Cesar learned fast. Eventually, Dolores was working as a lobbyist, convincing politicians to make laws that would help the farm workers. The CSO also pushed to get more Mexican-American police officers and more Spanish-speaking people at hospitals and government offices. They worked to get sewer systems and community centers in towns where the workers lived. The CSO was making a difference in people's lives. Dolores Huerta was part of this positive change.

ORGANIZING AND PARENTING

Dolores was working for the CSO when she met Ventura Huerta. They married and had five children together: Fidel, Emilio, Vincent, Alicia, and Angela. Dolores adored every one of her seven children, but she also loved her work.

Working for the CSO was not like having a regular nine-to-five office job. Instead, Dolores traveled all over the state of California, registering Mexican Americans to vote. She was often away from home for days at a time. When she traveled, she missed her family terribly. Still, she could not abandon the farm workers, either.

Unfortunately, Dolores paid a high price for her dedication. Because of her never-ending work with the CSO, her marriage to Ventura Huerta ended in divorce. They fought over who would get the children. Dolores won. Once again, Dolores's mother helped support her daughter's large family.

After years of working for the CSO, Cesar Chavez became frustrated. The changes he and Dolores had hoped for were not happening. Cesar was sure that only a union could solve the farm workers' problems. Alone, a single farm worker had little or no power. But working together, as a union, farm workers had a chance against the growers who hired them. Other kinds of workers in the United States had formed unions. Factory workers' unions had won benefits such as fair pay, paid vacations, sick leave, and better working conditions for their members. These were exactly the things that Cesar and Dolores knew farm workers deserved.

Cesar believed he could start a farm workers' union, and Dolores shared his faith. But Fred Ross and the CSO did not. They felt that it was too big a job. So in 1962, Cesar quit the CSO to start a farm workers' union. He and his wife, Helen, moved their family to Delano, California. Dolores was one of his most loyal supporters in his decision. She did not want her children to spend their lives as poor migrant workers, "looking down at the soil, picking crops," she said. "They should also look up to God." A farm workers' union, she believed, could help her children do that.

Soon after Cesar quit the CSO, Dolores also left. She joined Cesar and Helen in Delano. Together they began their work to start a farm workers' union. But they decided not to use the word "union." If growers heard that word, they might become angry and quickly fire all their workers. Instead, Cesar, Dolores, and Helen called their organization the National Farm Workers Association, or NFWA. Dolores was soon elected vice president.

At first, Dolores was worried about her children. Even though the NFWA gave her an allowance for food, clothing, and housing, her real pay was only five dollars a week! And a lot of her time was still spent traveling. Who would look after her children while she was away? Her own mother, Alicia, had stayed in Stockton when Dolores moved to Delano.

Luckily, the union came through for Dolores. Union

In the early 1960s Dolores and Cesar worked together to organize the first farm workers' union.

Dolores Huerta was dedicated both to her family and to her union, the National Farm Workers Association.

members helped each other out like a big family. When Dolores was not home, Cesar and Helen or other union members looked after her children. Other times, her older children helped take care of the younger ones.

Knowing that her children were well cared for, Dolores could focus on her work for the NFWA. Her first concern was getting enough money for the union to survive. Dolores and Cesar wanted this union to be democratic, meaning that the members voted on all important decisions. In order for union members to keep their power, they had to help supply the money. One way to do that was to pay dues. The NFWA decided to charge $3.50 a month. This may not seem like much, but farm workers often did not even have enough money for food. For them, $3.50 a month was a lot of money!

Dolores and Cesar set out to recruit, or bring in, members to the NFWA. Dolores worked the northern part of the Central Valley in California. Cesar worked the southern part. They drove from town to town talking to the farm workers. They had house meetings to organize people all over the state. It was not easy to convince people to join. Dolores and Cesar explained that by paying dues, each worker would have a voice in the NFWA.

All this recruitment work took time and money. It was difficult for Dolores, traveling and having almost no money, with seven children depending on her. But she was not the only one struggling. Cesar used up his savings and had to ask for food from the farm workers to help feed Helen, himself, and their eight children.

Finally, Dolores's and Cesar's hard work paid off. By 1964, the NFWA had signed up almost a thousand farm-worker families. Belonging to the NFWA had many benefits for members. The NFWA provided them with community service programs, life insurance, and a credit union, a sort of private bank. It also started a store that sold goods to members at a discount. These programs made the workers' lives easier. But the NFWA's most difficult work was still ahead.

In May 1965, workers at a rose nursery in Delano

came to the NFWA with a complaint. The nursery owner paid these workers less than he had promised when he hired them. Cesar and Dolores told the workers not to come to work again until the owner agreed to raise their pay. Dolores and Cesar were organizing their first **strike**!

A strike is a form of protest where workers refuse to work until their demands are met. People go on strike to get better pay, better working conditions, or changes in working hours. A strike is a powerful tool for unions. Owners can lose a lot of money if their workers refuse to do their jobs. But a strike works only if the workers stick together. If some people go to work, or if the owner can hire someone else to do the same job, then the strike can be broken.

After the meeting with the rose workers, Dolores was very happy. But Cesar was worried some workers would get scared and go to work anyway. So early the next morning, Cesar and Dolores drove around to the workers' homes to see if any of them were getting ready to go to work. All seemed quiet until they came to a house that was all lit up. Dolores jumped out of the NFWA truck. She was not going to let a few people ruin the strike. When the workers refused to listen to her, she backed the truck into their driveway and blocked the workers' car. The workers gave up and went back to bed. No one else reported to work that day, either.

The nursery owner was furious. He tried to hire

The strike became an important tool for the farm workers in their struggle for justice. The Aztec eagle was their symbol. In Spanish, the word for strike is *huelga*.

new help, but the people he hired were not skilled, and they ruined his delicate rose bushes. So the nursery owner finally agreed to pay his workers the amount he had originally promised. The strike was over after only four days. The National Farm Workers Association had won its first victory!

THE NATIONAL GRAPE BOYCOTT

The NFWA got a lot of attention after the successful rose workers' strike. It was an exciting time for Dolores Huerta and the union that she cofounded. Membership in the NFWA grew. Dolores and Cesar were feeling good as they continued their work. But they were not prepared for one event that would put their union to the test. In 1965, a group of grape pickers went on strike against a California vineyard. They asked the NFWA to join them. The NFWA had to decide whether to support the strikers by going out on strike themselves.

The NFWA held a rally. The members gathered together and voted to join the strike. The moment Dolores and Cesar had been preparing for all these years had finally arrived.

Instead of working in the fields, the strikers marched in a **picket line** outside the vineyard. They carried signs with their new symbol: a black eagle

Dolores Huerta talks with Mexican-American grape pickers. The strike gave new hope to the farm workers.

inside a white circle on a red background. The symbol was based on the Aztec eagle found on ancient buildings in Mexico. The Aztec people lived in Mexico long before the Europeans came to the New World. So the NFWA's new symbol had special meaning for the Mexican-American workers. It showed their culture, and it stood for hope and freedom for farm workers. The NFWA also had a slogan: *Viva La Causa*, which means "Long live the cause."

Dolores was a picket captain in charge of the picket lines. She marched in the roads beside the fields with hundreds of strikers. Some vineyard owners tried to break the strike. They brought in workers from Mexico, paying them less money to do the same work.

Dolores and Cesar saw that a strike might not work for the farm workers. The growers were getting the grapes picked without using any union workers. That meant the strike could last a very long time. Striking workers were unable to pay dues. Fortunately, the farm workers received contributions of food and supplies from non-members and volunteers.

It was a very difficult time for the farm workers. Not only were they giving up their jobs, they were also in danger much of the time. The growers were very powerful in the communities where the farm workers lived and worked. They secretly influenced the police departments and the courts. The growers hired men to beat up the workers. The police would not protect the union members. In fact, the police often arrested the workers for "disturbing the peace."

Although the NFWA's efforts were often met with violence, Cesar and Dolores did not want the workers to respond with violence. If that happened, Dolores said, "people would start killing each other and the killing would never end." But Cesar and Dolores could not place workers in dangerous situations where they were not allowed to defend themselves. It was a real problem for the NFWA.

Cesar and Dolores found a solution. They organized a **boycott**. A boycott is when people refuse to buy certain products or to shop at the stores that sell those

People all over the country supported the farm workers' union by joining the grape boycott. Here, Cesar Chavez marches with other boycott supporters outside a Miami supermarket.

products. The growers lose money because no one is buying what they have to sell. Yet the only way a boycott can work is if millions of people agree not to buy the products being boycotted. Dolores and Cesar set out to inform the people and ask them not to buy or sell grapes grown in California.

Most people who buy fruits and vegetables from a supermarket do not know how their food gets there. They often have no idea who picks the fruit or how the workers live. So, the NFWA had to get the word out. They did it the same way they ran the union—they let the farm workers speak for themselves. Many farm-working families packed up their things and headed to cities. There, they told people face-to-face what their lives were like, why they were on strike, and why everyone should support the boycott.

The boycott made the entire country aware of the farm workers' struggle. Across the country people stopped buying California wine or grapes. It was as if the American public had joined the strikers on the picket line. Sure, the growers could hire new workers to pick grapes, but they could not force the American public to buy their products.

In 1966, to make people aware of the boycott, Dolores and Cesar organized a 300-mile march from the union's main office in Delano, California, to the state capitol building in Sacramento. Dolores called the march a pilgrimage. A pilgrimage is a long journey, usually to a religious place. Like Dolores, most of the farm workers were very religious. She hoped this pilgrimage would give everyone in the union the moral strength to keep facing the hardships of their long strike.

About seventy marchers left Delano carrying posters and banners. They wanted everyone to know who they were and what they were protesting. Most of the marchers made it to the end—and it was worth every step! One of the growers had agreed to talk to the union.

Dolores was chosen to talk to the grower. It was her job to create a contract, or written agreement, that would be good for all the farm workers. Dolores had never even read a union contract, much less written one. But, she learned fast. The new contract raised the farm workers' **minimum wage** to $1.75 an hour. No union member could be paid less than that. Under the new agreement, workers could also earn paid holidays and vacations. They were also guaranteed days off. In addition, thanks to the union, farm workers now had unemployment insurance. This meant that when they were out of work, they would still receive some money to live on.

Cesar Chavez speaks from the steps of the California State Capitol at the end of the farm workers' 300-mile march.

Many other growers still refused to recognize the union and the rights of the workers. So the boycott continued. In 1968, Dolores went to New York to take charge of the boycott there. She did not know what to expect. "I thought, 11 million people in New York, and I have to persuade them to stop buying grapes!" Dolores stayed in New York for two years, organizing marches and rallies all over the city and in other cities as well. Millions of people marched with the farm workers to show their support for La Causa. Dolores made hundreds of speeches that brought in many new supporters. Because of her efforts, even the New York City government agreed to support the boycott and not to buy California grapes.

It was an exciting time, but it was not always easy for Dolores. Her family was once again split up. Some of her children came to New York with her, while others stayed in California. One daughter, Lori, traveled with Teatro Campesino, a Mexican-American theater group. The group's shows helped raise money for the boycott.

Dolores missed having her family together. She also missed being in California. But she was not the only one making sacrifices. The farm workers who had come with her to New York were also getting homesick. As the strike and boycott dragged on, everyone was becoming frustrated.

Cesar Chavez was a strong believer in the work of Mohandas K. Gandhi, who had helped the country of

Cesar Chavez (right) after twenty days of fasting in 1968.

India gain its independence from Great Britain in 1947. Gandhi believed in using nonviolent protest to bring about social change. Sometimes he would fast, or not eat, until people paid attention to his cause. Cesar decided he would fast, too. For 25 days, he ate nothing. His weight fell from 175 to 140 pounds.

Cesar's fast was in all the national newspapers. Politicians and movie stars came to visit him and voiced their support for La Causa. More importantly,

Dolores Huerta's powerful voice helped lead the farm workers to a victory in the grape boycott.

Cesar's fast impressed the workers themselves. They now saw that nonviolent protest could work.

By 1970, most of the vineyards were paying fair wages. This was a major victory for the union. It took five long years, but the union finally won. For Dolores Huerta it was a double victory because she was finally able to go back home to her children—at least for a little while.

THE STRUGGLE CONTINUES

The grape boycott victory was reason for celebration for the farm workers' union. Membership was booming. At its peak in the 1970s, the union had more than 100,000 members. The effects of the boycott moved beyond the union's own gains. The farm workers' union had shown the world that a boycott could work. They had given people a new way to fight for change nonviolently. Dolores believed that the boycott was also the first step in winning justice for farm workers everywhere. "It may not happen right now," she said, "but the pattern is there and farm workers are going to make it."

In 1972, the farm workers' union joined with the AFL-CIO, the most powerful labor union in the country. It became the United Farm Workers (UFW). Cesar Chavez was elected to serve as president of the UFW, and Dolores Huerta was elected vice president.

Dolores's personal life took a change for the better

when she married Richard Chavez, Cesar's brother. Finally, she was with a husband who shared her passion for the union and would not be jealous of the time she donated to La Causa. They had four children together: Juanita, Maria Elena, Ricky, and Camilla.

Dolores's work life, however, is still a challenge. After nearly thirty years of hard work with the union, many farm-working families still live in poverty. Farm workers remain some of the lowest-paid workers in America. Migrant workers often have no housing. Some live in their automobiles during the harvest season and have to bathe in ditches that are filled with polluted water. It is a very unhealthy way to live. Farm workers and their families sometimes get sick with malaria and tuberculosis.

It is the children who suffer the most. Families are forced to have their children work, to bring in enough money to survive. This makes it harder for the children to get the education they need. Without a good education, they cannot get a better job when they are older.

At one point, it also became clear that many farm workers' children were getting cancer. The UFW looked into the high rate of childhood cancer in several California communities. The union believes the cancers are caused by pesticides, which are chemicals sprayed over food crops to kill insects. But many pesticides are also poisonous for humans. Sometimes the workers are not even told they are working with

After more than thirty years, Dolores Huerta is still fighting for justice. Here, she leads a 1988 rally against the use of poisonous pesticides.

poisons. And even if they are told, they may be afraid to speak out for fear of losing their jobs. During the 1980s, Dolores often spoke before Congress, which makes national laws. She talked about pesticides and other health issues that farm workers have to face.

Dolores also continued to travel around the country, speaking with different groups in support of the farm workers. When the UFW held a new grape boycott in the 1980s, she helped to keep it going.

The day after Cesar Chavez's death in 1993, Dolores joined with other union leaders in a promise to carry on his work.

Dolores also helped to found the union's own radio station, Radio Campesina. (*Campesina* is a Spanish word for farm worker.)

The 1980s and early 1990s have brought many new challenges to Dolores Huerta's life and work. They also brought a tragedy. On April 23, 1993, Cesar

Chavez died of a heart attack. He was only 66 years old.

Often the death of a leader such as Chavez makes people think that the entire movement has died along with him. But Dolores would not allow this to happen to the union she founded with him. At his funeral, Dolores and other UFW leaders promised that the struggle would continue.

Today, the union is facing hard times. Most growers are again hiring non-union labor. Farm workers' wages and living conditions have become worse as the country struggles with its own economic problems. Some businesses and politicians are fighting harder than ever against unions. The UFW has also been weakened by problems of its own. But, as always, Dolores Huerta remains on the front line, fighting for farm workers' rights.

Dolores also continues to set a strong example for women like her everywhere. Dolores has always been an active feminist. Working with Cesar, she always made sure that women were in positions of power in the union. In fact, nearly half the UFW organizers are women. Important programs such as the credit union and the union's health clinic are run by women.

Dolores knows from firsthand experience how difficult it is for women to work for the union and take care of their children. She herself had 11 kids and was pregnant most of the time she was working. (In fact, between the oldest and youngest child there is a difference of 26 years.) While she was out helping

In 1993, Dolores Huerta was honored as a "Woman of Courage" by the National Organization for Women.

others, Dolores depended on union members to look after her own children. She often felt guilty for not spending more time with her children. "It's true, the kids resent it when the union takes time away from them," Dolores said in 1975. Now she is convinced, however, that her children gained a lot growing up the way they did. "I can look back and say it's okay because my kids turned out fine," she said.

Dolores is pleased with the paths her children have chosen as adults. Most of her children were involved with the union at some point in their lives.

But most have gone on with their own careers. One son is a doctor who takes time out to help the homeless. Another is a lawyer. One is a chef. One daughter is a nurse, and one still works for the union.

In a 1993 interview, Dolores said she hoped that women everywhere would begin to make their own decisions, in their families and their lives. She also hoped that women would take credit for the truly important work they do and believe strongly in themselves. Her own struggle against sexism and racism will continue, Dolores said. "I'll just keep going as long as I can and die with my boots on." Dolores Huerta is true to her word. She's still fighting strong for La Causa—hers and ours.

Important Dates

1930   Born Dolores Fernandez on April 10 in Dawson, New Mexico.

1936   Moves to Stockton, California, with her mother and brothers.

1955   Meets Fred Ross. Begins working for the Community Service Organization (CSO).

1962   Joins Cesar and Helen Chavez in Delano, California, to form a union called the National Farm Workers Association (NFWA).

1965   Helps organize grape pickers' strike and boycott against grapes.

1966   Marches from Delano to Sacramento with farm workers to publicize grape boycott.

1968   Goes to New York City to direct boycott effort there.

1970   Negotiates union contracts with many grape growers as a result of the success of the boycott.

1972   Elected vice president of the union, now called United Farm Workers (UFW).

1988   Protests in San Francisco against the policies of George Bush and is seriously injured by police.

1993   Vows to fight on for her beliefs after Cesar Chavez dies of a heart attack on April 23.

Glossary

boycott: A kind of protest in which the public refuses to buy certain products.

labor movement: The term used for labor unions working to improve labor conditions.

migrant workers: Farm workers who move from farm to farm to pick crops.

minimum wage: The lowest legal wage that can be paid to a worker.

picket line: A kind of protest where people march in line outside a business they are striking against.

strike: A kind of protest where people refuse to return to work until they are given better pay or working conditions.

working conditions: How workers are treated at their workplace.

Bibliography

Holmes, Burnham. *Cesar Chavez: Farm Worker Activist*. Austin, TX: Raintree Steck-Vaughn, 1994.

Morey, Janet. *Famous Mexican Americans*. New York: Dutton, 1989.

Roberts, Maurice. *Cesar Chavez and La Causa*. Chicago: Childrens Press, 1986.

Index